Birthday Cake

Ch...

Monster
Mash

Chicken Biscuits

Mitey Oats

Crispy Chicken

Coconut Biscuits

Chicken Barley

Crispy Beef

Crispy Sweet Potato

i Burgers

its

Homemade **Dog Treats**

Recipe Book

Wet Nose
Publishing Ltd

First published in November 2016 by **Wet Nose Publishing Ltd**
email cdw@wetnosepublishing.co.uk
www.countrysidedogwalks.co.uk
ISBN 978-0-9931923-7-1

We would like to thank Nicki Crawley BSc Dip ACNS Cert AAH Nutrtional Advisor

Text and photographs © Wet Nose Publishing Ltd 2016
All rights reserved. This publication must not be reproduced in any form without prior written permission from the publisher.
British Library Cataloguing-in-publication data.
A catalogue is available for this book from the British Library.
Whilst every effort has been made to ensure that the information in this book is correct, the author or the publisher can accept no responsibility for errors, loss or injury however caused.
Printed in Poland
www.lfbookservices.co.uk

Useful Tips

* Don't eat the ingredients
* Share wih local hounds
* Check all instructions
* Keep cats away
* Work as a team
* Keep paws clean
* Stash everything
* Don't chew utensils
* Leave no evidence
* Dribble sparingly
* Have fun - chase a cat!
* Keep your fleas out
* Remember, I'm the boss
* Lend a helping paw
* Don't let the humans know what we are doing!

Fridge raided, now for a nap!

Contents

Introduction

All dogs deserve to have healthy foods. Do you worry about what goes into your dog's treats? Can you be sure that all the ingredients are listed? There have been so many scares on social media about what substances are in dog foods and treats, so why not make natural, healthy and nutritious treats for your best friend.

All the recipes in this book have been designed so that they are quick and easy to prepare, using everyday all-natural ingredients. There are step-by-step instructions that have been followed by a complete novice, who had never baked before. We have used a nutritionist to check all the ingredients in our recipes to make sure that they are safe for dogs to eat. If you have a dog with a sensitive stomach, we have some recipes that are gluten free, and are marked clearly.

We hope the book will bring lots of fun along the way, as you begin to bake treats for your dog. There are lots of coloured photos, where we have humanised the dogs to make it look as though they have done all the baking. It's a dog's world.

Treat your dog

The recipes are for the purpose of treating your dog only, and not part of your dog's daily balanced diet. It is important that treats are only given sparingly. If you are using treats whilst training your dog, and therefore feeding more than usual, reduce the amount of daily dog food to avoid your dog gaining excess weight.

No Preservatives

As there are no preservatives, the treats won't last as long as shop bought treats. You can simply freeze a batch of them for another day. Don't defrost all the treats at once, only what you intend to feed for a couple of days.

Let the treats cool

It's important to let the treats cool down completely before you put them into an airtight container. If they are still slightly warm, then condensation will build up and the treats will go soggy, which will also reduce the longevity of the treat. The treats may feel cold to touch, but may still be warm inside. It's best to leave them for at least a couple of hours.

Don't be afraid to make changes

Sometimes when you follow a recipe, you can find that your dough is too wet and sticky, or too dry and therefore not binding together. If it's too wet, just add a few more dry ingredients (flour if this is in your recipe). If it's too dry add a drop of water or milk, until you have the desired consistency. You can also change the amount of ingredients to make more or less, as long as you keep the ratio the same.

Tried and tested

All the treats have been given to a great number of dogs at local shows, and they all loved them. The dogs in the Wet Nose Publishing team (see below in About Us) have had these treats regularly and along with their all-natural daily dog food they are thriving very well.

Poisonous foods you must avoid

Thankfully information is available these days to ensure we feed our dogs well. Throughout this book we have strictly adhered to wholesome natural ingredients. Below is a basic list of foods and food products to avoid giving to your dog.

Chocolate
Grapes – including raisins, sultanas and currants
Onions, garlic, shallots and chives
Macadamia nuts

Avocado
Xylitol – This is an artificial sweetener, which can be used in all sorts of foods. Peanut butter can contain this sweetener, so always check when you buy peanut butter to use as an ingredient for making dog treats, that it doesn't contain this substance.

About us

Wet Nose Publishing Ltd was formed in 2012. Included in the team (at time of writing) are five dogs - Belay, Ozark, Pebbles, Bokeh and Frazzle. There is also two humans. We have owned dogs throughout our lives, and are a little dog crazy (well maybe a lot). Our dogs have a great outdoor life (when they are not lazing around on the sofa), as they take part in creating our Dog Friendly walking books. They have walked all the walks in our 17 books (currently) twice!! They also have great dog walking areas where we live. They need to be fit and healthy, and they are thriving on their daily dog food and the treats (given sparingly), which are included in this book. Their daily food is an all-natural dried food made by CSJ - http://www.csjk9.com/, as we believe 'You are what you eat'.

1. Mince Pockets

Ingredients

- 4oz - 113g - ¾ cup self raising wholemeal flour
- 2oz - 57g - ⅓ cup Butter/Margarine
- 1 tablespoon of water
- 2oz - 57g - ⅓ cup minced beef/lamb
- A drop of milk

Oven temperature and cooking times

160°c / 325°f / Gas mark 3 for 15 to 20 minutes (reduce the time for fan assisted ovens)

"Are they done yet?"

Method

To make a pastry: -
Sift the flour into a mixing bowl
Add the butter/margarine and fold into the flour with a knife
Mix with your fingertips until it looks like breadcrumbs
Add the water and mix with a knife
Bring it all together using your hands and knead into the bowl until the bowl is clean
Sprinkle flour onto a surface and roll out the dough thinly (2mm)
Using a round pasty cutter or an egg cup, cut out an even amount of shapes and place half on a greased baking tray
Using a pastry brush (or your finger), add a coating of milk, making sure you include the edges
Add the mince onto the pastry and then use the remaining shapes, make lids, and pinch the edges together to seal

Cook in a pre heated oven, until golden brown

Leave to cool on a wire tray. When the treats are completely cold they can be frozen or stored in an airtight container.

Makes 15 treats

"Are they having a laugh?"

2. Mitey Oats

Ingredients

- 8oz - 226g - 2 cups of rolled oats
- 1 medium free range egg
- 2 fluid oz - 60ml - ¼ cup of water
- 1 teaspoon of yeast extract – e.g. Marmite or Vegemite

Oven Temperature and Cooking Times

160°c / 325°f / Gas mark 3 for 30 minutes (reduce the time for fan assisted ovens)

Method

Put all the ingredients into a bowl
Mix together until the yeast extract adds a fairly even tint, leaving no visible white oats
If necessary add extra drops of water gradually, until all the oats bind together
Pinch a bit of the mixture off, and knead together between both finger and thumbs, turning the mixture as you do it to create a shape of a lozenge
The ideal size 2cm diameter and 1.5cm thick.
If the mixture won't bind together, then leave to stand for 15 minutes and try again, as some oats take longer to soak up the water

Cook in a pre-heated oven, and then cool on a wire rack.

Store in an airtight container for up to five days, or freeze on the day of baking.

Makes 50 treats

Dishwashing Team

3.Weightless Wonders (Gluten Free)

Ingredients

- 2 florets of broccoli (raw)
- 4oz - 113g - ½ cup of rice
- a ½ carrot (raw and unpeeled)
- 1 free range egg

Oven Temperature and Cooking Times

160°c / 325°f / Gas mark 3 for 30 minutes (reduce the time for fan assisted ovens)

Method

Boil the rice until cooked, rinse in cold water, and drain
Finely chop the broccoli, and grate the carrot
Place all the ingredients into a mixing bowl and stir together, ensuring that it is well mixed
Grease a 12-segment bun/cake tray, or use small foil tart cases
Divide the mixture evenly into the tray or 12 tart cases, and compact with the back of a teaspoon

Cook in a pre-heated oven. Once cooked turn off the oven and take out the treats, keeping the oven door closed. Gently loosen the treats using a teaspoon and transfer onto a wire cooling rack. Pop them back in the oven on the rack, with the oven switched off, but using the heat to dry the treats out and leave until cold.

Store in an airtight container for up to 3 days, or freeze on the day of baking and store them in a plastic container to prevent them breaking.

Makes 12 treats

Master Chef

4. Honey Bites

Ingredients

- 5oz - 140g - ¾ cup self raising flour
- 4oz - 113g - 1 cup rolled oats
- 1oz - 28g - ⅓ cup desiccated coconut
- 4oz - 113g - ½ cup butter/margarine
- 2 tablespoons honey
- 1 level teaspoon bicarbonate soda
- 1 tablespoon milk

Oven Temperature and cooking times

180°c / 350°f / Gas mark 4 Bake for 15 minutes (reduce the time for fan assisted ovens)

Method

Combine flour, oats and coconut into a mixing bowl
Stir together
Put butter/margarine and honey into a saucepan and mix on a very low heat, stirring continuously until melted into a liquid and then take off the heat
Mix the milk with the bicarbonate of soda and add to the honey liquid
Stir the liquid into the mixing bowl until completely mixed together
Cover with a clean tea towel and leave to stand for around 15-20 minutes
Grease two baking trays
Divide the mixture into small balls – size of a marble and space well on the baking trays
Put into a preheated oven and bake until golden brown. Once done, turn off the oven, open the oven door to release any steam and then close the door and use the remaining heat in the oven to allow treats to dry out.

When the treats are completely cold they can be frozen or stored in an airtight container.

Makes 30

"Quick - run!"

5. Liver Biscuits

Ingredients

- 8oz - 226g - ½lb of lamb's liver
- 1 carrot
- 1 stick of celery
- 8oz - 226g - 2 cups wholemeal flour
- 2 tablespoons of water

Oven temperature and cooking times

180°c / 350°f / Gas mark 4 Bake for 30 minutes (reduce the time for fan assisted ovens)

Method

Mince the lamb and the celery in a blender and put into a mixing bowl

Rinse the blender with the water (blend on the wash setting), and then put the water into the mixing bowl

Grate the carrot into the mixing bowl and stir well

Sieve the flour and fold into the ingredients gradually with a metal spoon, until dough is forming

Knead the dough in the bowl until the bowl becomes clean. You can add more flour if needed.

Sprinkle a clean work surface with flour

Roll out the dough to about 1 cm and cut out with a pastry cutter

Put the pastry shapes onto a greased baking tray

Cook in a preheated oven

Once cooked turn off the oven, open the oven door to allow steam to escape, and then leave in the oven until cold

The treats can be put into the freezer for up to 3 months. Once defrosted they must be eaten within three days, and kept in an airtight container

"The neighbours are here!"

6. Turmeric Biscuits

Ingredients

- 6oz - 170g - 1 cup of cooked brown rice*
- 6oz - 170g - 1 cup of cooked and mashed butternut squash*
- 2 eggs
- 12oz - 340g - 2½ cups of self-raising wholemeal flour
- 2 teaspoons of turmeric
- I tablespoon of olive oil
- 1 teaspoon of freshly ground black pepper (12 grounds)
- * If you have cooked too much rice or butternut squash you can freeze it

Oven temperature and cooking times

160°c / 325°f / Gas mark 3 for 20 minutes (reduce the time for fan assisted ovens)

Method

Boil the rice until cooked

Peel and chop the butternut squash into cubes and cook until tender and then mash

Put all the ingredients (except flour) into a mixing bowl and stir well

Mix the flour gradually and then using your hands make a firm dough (add more flour if necessary)

Sprinkle a clean surface with flour

Roll the dough out until it is roughly 1cm thick

Cut out shapes with a pastry cutter, or use an egg cup or glass

Put shapes onto a greased baking tray and put into a preheated oven

Once cooked turn off the oven, open the oven door to allow steam to escape, and then leave in the oven until cold

The treats can be put in the freezer or they will last 3-4 days in an aiftight container

Caught in the act!

7. Blueberry and Banana balls

Ingredients

- 2oz - 56g - ¼ cup blueberries
- 4oz - 113g - 1 cup of rolled oats
- 1 banana
- 5oz - 140g - 1 cup of wholemeal self raising flour
- 4 fluid oz -120ml - ½ cup of water

Oven temperature and cooking time

160°c / 325°f / Gas mark 3 for 30 minutes (reduce the time for fan assisted ovens)

Method

Mash the banana and blueberries in a mixing bowl
Add all the other ingredients
Mix the ingredients together using a metal spoon
Sprinkle a little more flour if necessary and form moist dough
Divide the dough to make balls roughly 2cm in diameter
Place on a greased oven tray and put into a preheated oven
Once cooked turn off the oven, open the oven door and allow steam to escape
Leave in the oven until cold

The treats can be put into the freezer or they will last for up to 4 days in an airtight container

Makes 18 treats

8. Peanut Crunch

Ingredients

- 8oz - 210g - 1½ cups wholemeal flour
- 1.5oz - 35gm - ¼ cup cornmeal/Polenta
- 1oz - 30gm - ¼ cup of rolled oats
- 6 fluid oz - 170ml - ¾ cup of water
- 1 tablespoon of olive oil
- 1 egg
- 2 tablespoons of peanut butter (must not contain Xylitol)

Oven temperature and cooking times

200°c / 400°f / Gas mark 6 for 25 minutes (reduce the time for fan assisted ovens)

Method

Mix the flour, cornmeal and oats into a mixing bowl

Make a well in the centre and add the water, oil, peanut butter and the eggs

Mix all the ingredients together, and with your hands make into dough until the bowl is clean

Sprinkle a clean surface with flour

Roll out the dough until it is 1cm thick, and then cut out shapes with a pastry cutter or egg cup

Place on a greased baking tray and cook in a preheated oven

Once cooked turn off the oven, open the door briefly to allow steam to escape and then leave in the warm oven until cold

The treats can be put into the freezer. Once defrosted keep in an airtight container and consume within 4 days

9. Sardine Swirls

Ingredients

- 10oz - 280g - 2 cups of strong white flour
- 1 sachet of easy bake dried yeast
- 8 fluid oz - 227ml - 1 cup of warm water
- a ¼ cup of sunflower seeds
- 2 x 120g tins of sardines

Oven temperature and times

160°c / 325°f / Gas mark 3 for 30 minutes (reduce the time for fan assisted ovens)

"I said PASS me some eggs!"

Method

Sieve the flour into a mixing bowl

Add the yeast and the sunflower seeds and mix together

Gradually add the water, and mix to a dough

If the dough is too sticky, add a little more flour

Knead the dough on a clean flour-dusted surface for ten minutes

Divide the dough into two, and then roll out each one to form a rectangle, roughly 12cm wide, 25cm long and 5mm thick

Mash the sardines with a fork and then spread evenly onto each

Keep the length of each and roll the dough up (width to width) to form a sausage shape

Cut slices of about 1cm thick pieces

Place flat onto a greased baking tray

Leave for about 15 minutes in a warm place to proof (in the oven on the lowest setting will do)

Place in a pre-heated oven for around 30 minutes

Switch off the oven, open the oven door to allow steam to be released and then leave in the oven, to go cold and dry out

Oven guard duty

10. Chicken Dips

Ingredients

- 1 chicken breast
- 2 tablespoons of plain flour
- 1 large egg
- 2oz - 60g - 1½ cups of bran flakes or bread crumbs

Oven temperature and times

180°c / 350°f / Gas mark 4 Bake for 30 minutes (reduce the time for fan assisted ovens)

"Who gets the last one?"

Method

Crush the bran flakes into small crumbs

Cut the raw chicken breast with scissors, into strips about the size of your little finger

Beat the egg with a fork and place into a small dish

Place the flour into another small dish

Place the crushed bran flakes into a dish

Dip each chicken strip into the flour and then the egg, and then dip into the bran flakes/bread crumbs until covered all over

Place on a greased baking tray

Cook for 30 minutes and then turn off the oven, allow steam to be released by opening and closing the oven door, and then leave in the oven to go cold

The treats can be put into the freezer for up to 3 months. Defrosted or fresh treats should be eaten within 3 days and kept in an airtight container in the fridge

"Sorry, we don't open til 8…another 5 minutes yet"

11. Peanut Sesame Treats

Ingredients

- 8oz - 226g - 1½ cups of self-raising flour
- 1 teaspoon of dried or freshly chopped parsley
- 3oz - 85g - ⅓ cup of margarine
- 3oz - 85g - ⅓ cup of sesame seeds
- 3 tablespoons of milk
- Peanut butter (must not contain Xylitol)

Oven temperature and times

190°c / 375°f / Gas 5 for 20 minutes

Method

Sieve the flour into a mixing bowl

Stir in sesame seeds and parsley and then add the margarine

Mix the ingredients together, until they resemble fine breadcrumbs

Add the milk and bring together to form dough

Knead the dough on a clean-floured surface until smooth

Divide the dough into two

Roll out the dough with your hands into two sausage shapes

Slice the dough (about 1cm thick)

Spread the peanut butter onto each slice

Place slices (with the peanut butter on the top) onto a greased oven tray

Bake for 30 minutes, turn oven off and open the oven door briefly to allow steam to escape

Leave in oven to dry out and go cold

The treats can be put into the freezer. Once defrosted keep in an airtight container and consume within 4 days

"Oh no, did I just see a hair in the pastry?"

12. Liver cake

Ingredients

- 8oz - 225g - ½lb lamb or ox liver
- 10oz - 280g - 2 cups of self-raising wholemeal flour
- 1 egg
- Milk or water

Oven temperature and cooking times

180°c / 350°f / Gas mark 4 for 35 – 45 minutes

Method

Crack the eggs into a measuring jug

Add an equal volume of milk or water to the measuring jug and whisk

Blitz the liver in a blender

Add the egg, flour and blended liver into a large mixing bowl and stir thoroughly

Empty the contents into a greased baking tray and spread out evenly

Bake in a preheated oven

Allow to cool, cut into four even pieces and then tease out of tray using a frying spatula

Cut the four pieces into four again

Can be frozen for up to 3 months, store defrosted pieces in an airtight container for up to 3 days

Tools at the ready

13. Mini Burgers

Ingredients

- 5oz - 140gm - 1 cup of wholemeal flour
- 4oz - 113gm - 1 cup of rolled oats
- 12oz - 340g - 2 cups of minced lamb/beef
- 1 egg
- 5 green beans or 2oz - 60g - ⅓ cup garden peas
- 1 large carrot
- 1 apple
- 4 fluid oz - 120ml - a ½ cup of water if needed

Oven temperature and cooking times

180°c / 350°f / Gas mark 4 Bake for 45 minutes (reduce for fan assisted ovens)

Method

Chop the apple and the green beans (if using) into small pieces

Grate the carrot

Put all the ingredients into a large mixing bowl

Mix the ingredients together really well, until the ingredients are mixed evenly

You should have a fairly sticky mixture. If the mixture is too dry add a little water a little at a time, or if it's too wet add a little extra flour

Using a teaspoon, take out heaped quantities of the mixture

Press with your finger to compact any loose ingredients together

Push the mixture off the spoon with your finger, onto a greased baking tray leaving small gaps in between

Cook until golden brown

Turn the oven off when they are cooked and open the oven door to release any steam

Leave in the closed oven to dry out and go cold

Makes around 30 – 50 depending on size

The treats can be put into the freezer. Once defrosted keep in an airtight container and consume within 4 days

"Why does she get more?"

14. Crispy Beef, Chicken or Sweet Potato (Gluten Free

Ingredients

- Cubes of stewing steak or sliced strips of chicken breast or sweet potato (or all three)

Oven temperature and cooking times

190°c / 375°f / Gas 5 for one to three hours, depending on size of cubes

Method

Cut the cubed steak into three to save on cooking time, alternatively slice raw chicken breast or raw sweet potato into strips

Place on a baking tray and cook in the oven for at least an hour

During the cooking process, open the oven to release any steam

The idea is to bake the meat/potato to dry the pieces out until they go hard and crispy

If you are cooking a large joint of meat at the same time, and therefore will have your oven on for up to three hours, you can put the cubes of steak in whole and cook longer

After they are fully baked release any steam out of the oven, turn the oven off and leave in the oven until cold

The treats will last for up to three months stored in an airtight container

Rule No.1 - Don't eat the ingredients!

15. Red Balls

Ingredients

- 12oz - 350g - 2½ cups plain flour
- 2 tsp. - ⅛ cup of sunflower seeds
- 1 beetroot
- 2oz - 56gm - ½ cup of rolled oats
- 1 egg
- 16oz - 453gm - 2 cups of cooked red lentils

Oven temperature and cooking times

190°c / 375°f / Gas 5 for 30 minutes

Method

Sieve the flour into a large mixing bowl
Add the sunflower seeds and rolled oats
Mix together
Add the cooked lentils and raw egg
Grate the raw beetroot and add into the mixing bowl
Mix all the ingredients together until you have a soft dough
Pinch small amounts of the dough and roll into a ball, about the size of a cherry tomato
Place on a baking tray and put into a pre-heated oven
Once cooked, switch the oven off, open the door briefly to allow any steam to be released and then leave in the warm oven until cold.

Can be kept in the freezer for up to 3 months, or in an airtight container for up to four days.

Makes roughly 26 treats

16. Marmite biscuits

Ingredients

- 6oz - 175g - 1¼ cups of wholemeal flour
- 4oz - 100g - ½ cup butter
- 2 teaspoons of honey
- 1 teaspoon of yeast extract - marmite/vegemite

Oven temperature and cooking times

150°c / 302°f / Gas mark 2 for 25 minutes

Method

Place butter and honey into a mixing bowl
Mix until light and fluffy
Add the flour and yeast extract and mix using your hands
Once dough is formed, roll out onto a floured surface until the dough is about 4mm thick
Cut into shapes and place on a greaseproof tray
Pop into a pre-heated oven

Can be kept in the freezer for up to 3 months or in an airtight container for up to 4 days

Makes 20 – 30 treats, depending on the size of cutter

All clean now!

17. Monster Mash

Ingredients

- 1 egg
- 450g - 1lb potatoes
- 2oz - 57g - ½ cup semolina
- 2 carrots
- 1 red pepper
- 1oz - 28gm - ¼ cup flax seeds
- 1oz - 28gm - ⅓ cup ground whole peanuts – not salted or roasted (ground easily using a blender)
- 1oz - 28gm - ⅛ cup pumpkin seeds
- 1oz - 28gm - ⅛ cup sunflower seeds
- 1 knob of butter or margarine

Oven temperature and cooking times

180°c / 356°f / Gas mark 4 for 30 minutes

Method

Cut the potatoes into halves or quarters without peeling them. Boil until cooked
Dice carrots leaving the skin on, and dice the red pepper
Add the seeds, peanut, carrots, pepper and egg into a large mixing bowl
Mix together
Mash the cooked potato adding a knob of butter or margarine, and stir into the mixing bowl a bit at a time
Divide the mixed ingredients with a tablespoon into two small cupcake/bun tray, or use paper tart cases on a baking tray

(for small dogs use a teaspoon to divide the ingredients and reduce cooking time)

Place into a pre-heated oven and cook until golden brown

Makes 18 treats

"When these cool down, they're all mine"

18. Fetchy Fruit

Ingredients

- 2 Bananas
- 1 Apple
- 4oz - 113g - 1 cup semolina
- a ½ tsp. fennel seeds
- 1 tsp. flax seeds
- 1 tsp. pumpkin seeds

Oven temperature and cooking times

180°c / 356°f / Gas mark 4 for 20-30 minutes

Method

Add the seeds and semolina into a large mixing bowl and stir together
Grate the whole apple into the mixing bowl, avoiding the core
Mash the bananas with a fork and add to the mixture
Stir the ingredients together until evenly mixed through
Using a teaspoon as a measure, take out quantities and spoon onto a greaseproof oven tray with small spaces in-between, until you have used up all the mixture. Alternatively you can use a piping bag and pipe out even quantities about 2cm in diameter
Once cooked, open the oven door to allow any steam to be released and then leave in the oven to go cold and dry out

Place into an airtight container. The treats will keep for several days or they can be kept for about 3 months in the freezer.

Makes roughly 22 treats

"I need BIG treats!"

19. Chicken Biscuits

Ingredients

- 1 sweet potato
- 1 chicken breast
- 5oz - 140gm - 1 cup wholemeal flour
- 2oz - 70gm - ½ cup polenta
- 1 egg
- 2oz - 56gm - ½ cup rolled oats
- 2 fluid ounces - 60ml - ¼ cup of water

Oven temperature and cooking times

160°c / 325°f / Gas mark 3 for 15 to 20 minutes (reduce the time for fan assisted ovens)

Method

Dice the chicken breast and blitz into a paste using a blender
Place the flour, polenta and rolled oats into a mixing bowl
Using a cheese grater, grate the unpeeled raw sweet potato into the mixing bowl
Stir the ingredients together and then add the chicken, water and egg
Knead into dough
Roll out onto a floured surface to about 1cm thick
Cut out shapes using a pastry cutter
When baked, turn off the oven and open the door to allow steam to be released. Close door and then leave until they are cold and dried out

Keep in an airtight container in the fridge for up to 4 days or freeze for up to 3 months

"Mmmmm…can't see any treats in here!"

20. Beef Risotto

Ingredients

- 2oz - 56gm - ½ cup of garden peas
- 10oz - 285g - ⅔lb of raw minced beef
- 12oz - 340g - 2 cups of cooked Arborio rice (risotto)
- 2oz - 57g - ⅓ cup polenta

Oven temperature and cooking times

180°c / 356°f / Gas mark 4 for 45 minutes

Method

Add all the ingredients into a large mixing bowl

Stir thoroughly until all the ingredients are evenly distributed

Using a tablespoon divide the mixture evenly into a 12-segmented cup cake tray

If you want to make smaller treats, then use a teaspoon and divide the mixture into even dollops onto a baking tray

Makes 12 large treats

"Who wanted the flour?"

21. Chicken Barley

Ingredients

- 12oz - 340g - 2 cups cooked barley
- 6oz - 170g - 1 cup semolina
- 1 chicken breast
- 1 tablespoon of pumpkin seeds
- 2 teaspoons of flax seeds

Oven temperature and cooking times

180°c / 356°f / Gas mark 4 for 35 minutes

Method

Blitz the chicken in a blender to form a paste, and then put into a large mixing bowl

Add the rest of the ingredients and mix together well, until the ingredients are combined

Take small amounts of the mixture and roll into balls

Place balls onto a greased baking tray

Cook until golden brown

Once cooked turn off the oven, open the oven door to allow any steam to escape, and then leave them in the oven to dry out and go cold

The treats can be frozen for up to 3 months. Once defrosted store them in an airtight container for up to three days

"We've made it!"

22. Cheddar Delight

Ingredients

- 4oz - 113g - ¼lb of cheddar cheese
- 2 eggs
- 5oz - 140g - 1 cup wholemeal flour
- 2oz - 56g - ⅓ cup polenta
- 1 heaped teaspoon sesame seeds
- 1 teaspoon freshly ground pepper
- 2 heaped teaspoons sunflower seeds
- 1 carrot

Oven temperature and cooking times

160°c / 325°f / Gas mark 3 for 15 to 20 minutes (reduce the time for fan assisted ovens)

Method

Add the flour, polenta and seeds into a large mixing bowl
Mix together well
Grate the cheese and uncooked/unpeeled carrot into the bowl
Add the eggs and mix together well, using your hands to make dough
Lightly flour a work surface
Place the dough onto the surface, put a sheet of greaseproof paper onto the dough and roll out until about 1cm thickness
Cut out shapes using pastry cutters or a small glass/egg cup

Once cooked release the steam and leave in the oven to cool a little
When the treats have cooled a little remove from the oven (keep the oven door closed) loosen them on the tray and then put them back in the oven to cool down completely

Makes 30 treats (depending on size of cutter)

Place cold treats into an airtight container, where they will keep for 4 to 5 days
Alternatively you can freeze for up to three months

23. Digestive Nibbles

Ingredients

- 4oz - 113g - 1 cup rolled oats
- 5oz - 140g - 1 cup wholemeal flour
- 1 teaspoon baking powder
- 1 teaspoon dried or finely chopped parsley
- 4oz - 100g - ¼lb butter/margarine
- 1-2 tablespoons of milk
- a ½ teaspoon of yeast extract (Marmite or Vegemite for example)

Oven temperature and cooking times

160°c / 325°f / Gas mark 3 for 15 to 20-25 minutes (reduce the time for fan assisted ovens)

Method

Blitz the oats to a fine powder using a blender

Place the oat powder, flour, parsley and baking powder into a large mixing bowl

Mix the ingredients together well

Add the butter/margarine and the yeast extract into the bowl, and mix together using your fingertips until it resembles a crumbly mixture

Add a tablespoon of milk and press the ingredients together until you form dough

If the mixture won't combine properly add another tablespoon of milk

Place the dough onto a lightly-floured surface and roll out, using a sheet of greaseproof paper on the top to prevent the dough sticking to the rolling pin

Cut out using pastry shape cutters, or a glass or egg cup, and place onto a greased baking tray and place in a preheated oven

When baked, turn off the oven and open the door, to allow steam to be released. Close the oven door and then leave until they are cold and dried out

The biscuits can be kept in an airtight container for 4 to 5 days or you can freeze for up to 3 months

Makes 40 biscuits (depending on the size of your pastry cutter)

24. Coconut Biscuits (Gluten Free)

Ingredients

- 2 bananas
- 2oz - 56g - ½ cup coconut flour
- 8oz - 227g - 2 cups flaked rice
- 2 free range eggs
- 1 tablespoon honey

Oven temperature and cooking times

180°c / 356°f / Gas mark 4 for 20 - 30 minutes (reduce the time for fan assisted ovens)

Method

Mash the bananas into a large mixing bowl

Add all other ingredients and stir together well

Transfer the mixture evenly into a 12-cupcake baking tray

Using a teaspoon, compact the mixture evenly into the segments

If you have any left over mixture, you will need to use two trays

Place into a preheated oven and cook until golden brown

When baked, turn off the oven and open the door to allow steam to be released. Close door and then leave until they are cold and dried out

Place in an airtight container and freeze. Treats will last for up to 3 days once defrosted.

Makes 15 treats

25. Birthday Cake

Ingredients

- 5oz - 140g - 1 cup self raising flour
- 4oz - 113g - ½ cup mince lamb/beef
- 1 chicken breast
- 2 eggs
- 2 fluid oz - 60ml - ¼cup of water

Oven temperature and cooking times

180°c / 356°f / Gas mark 4 for 25-30 minutes

Method

Blitz the mince and chicken together in a blender

Place into a large mixing bowl

Add the rest of the ingredients

Using the water, wash the blender and then add to the mixture

Stir well with a wooden spoon for 5-10 minutes until the mixture is light and fluffy

Place the mixture into a small loaf/cake tin and spread out evenly

Cook in a preheated oven

After the allotted time, place a skewer into the cake. If the skewer is clean, then the cake is done

Place on a cooling rack

When the cake is completely cold, you can transfer into a cake tin/airtight container or you can freeze for up to 3 months

Makes one small cake

Gilly

Meg

Jimmy Choo

Ava

Our Tasters and Models

Chandon

Romeo

Pebbles

Moet

Paddy

Milly

Betsi

Baxter

Toby

Sam

Piglet

Brook

Berty

Jess

Nellie

Crystal

Brennig

Brillo

Ozark

Blue

Frazzle

Eddy

Roger

Trixie

Percy

Molly

Ollie

Poppy

Mandy

Archie

Bokeh

Charlie

Molly

Chanel

Frank

Belay

More books available by Wet Nose Publishing Ltd

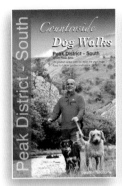
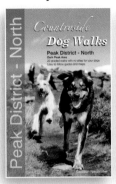
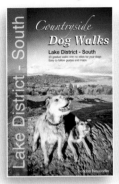
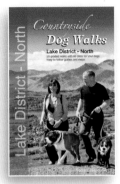

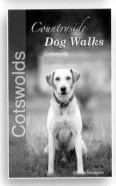

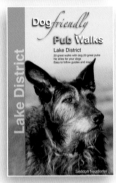

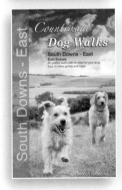
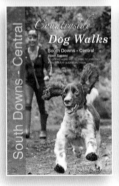
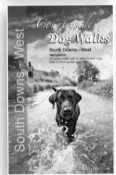

www.countrysidedogwalks.co.uk

Follow us on Facebook for progress reports on our future publications.

Search - Countryside Dog Walks